D0178061

Kids' Cook Book

Kids' Cook Book

Written by Pamela Gwyther
Photography by Mark Wood

p

With special thanks to our models Sophie Collins, Zion Duharty, Fran Eames and Kristal Lau

Home economist: Pamela Gwyther

This is a Parragon book
This edition published in 2006
Copyright © Parragon Books Ltd 2005
All rights reserved
ISBN 1-40548-070-X
Printed in China

Contents

4–6   number of
       servings

45   preparation
minutes   time

10   cooking
minutes   time

60   chilling
       time
minutes

The Magic of Cooking

Everyone enjoys eating delicious food, but cooking it
can be even more fun. Cooking is a kind of magic.
Just see how in a couple of hours you can change
a piece of raw dough into a tray of warm,
mouth-watering bread rolls!

To be a good cook, you need to get everything
ready in the kitchen before you start. Follow the recipe
steps carefully, and make sure you use your cooking
equipment in the right way. Take a few minutes to
read these pages, and then you'll be ready to
GET COOKING!

WEIGHING AND MEASURING

- A recipe will work much better if you weigh or
  measure your ingredients accurately. Guessing
  is not a good idea!

- Use kitchen weighing scales to measure out dry
  ingredients such as flour and sugar.

- Use a measuring jug for liquids – make sure
  you place the jug on a flat surface to measure
  accurately.

SAFETY FIRST

- Look out for the ⚠ symbol in the recipes. When you see this you need to ask for adult help to:
  - move food in and out of a hot oven
  - cook on the hob
  - use a sharp knife
  - use an electrical appliance such as a blender or a food processor.

- Always wear oven gloves when handling hot dishes, tins and trays.
- Remember to switch off your oven when you have finished cooking.
- When cooking on a hob, turn the pan handle to one side to avoid the heat. It also makes it harder to knock the pan off accidentally.
- Hold a saucepan handle steady with one hand while you stir.
- Always put hot pans on a heatproof mat or trivet when you remove them from the hob.
- Always chop or cut food on a chopping board, not your work surface.
- Keep sharp knives in a knife block or a safety wrapper when not in use.
- Never walk around with a sharp knife in your hand.
- Make sure your hands are dry when plugging and unplugging electrical equipment.
- Wipe up any spills on the floor straight away.

CLEAN AND TIDY

- Always wash your hands before you start to cook. When making pastry or bread, scrub your nails clean.
- Roll up your sleeves and always wear an apron.
- Tie your hair back if it's long.
- Make sure work surfaces and equipment are clean.
- Use clean tea towels. Keep a different towel to dry your hands.
- Wash your chopping board and knife in between different uses, especially after cutting up raw meat.

Cooking Things

1 electric blender

2 scale

3 food processor

4 grater

5 tongs

6 electric hand mixer

7 beaters

8 freezer box

9 electric hand
  blender

10 balloon whisk

1 pans

2 colander

3 cake tin

4 bun tin

5 baking sheet

6 mixing bowl

7 sifter

8 measuring jug

9 lemon squeezer

10 rolling pin

11 oven mitts

12 cooling rack

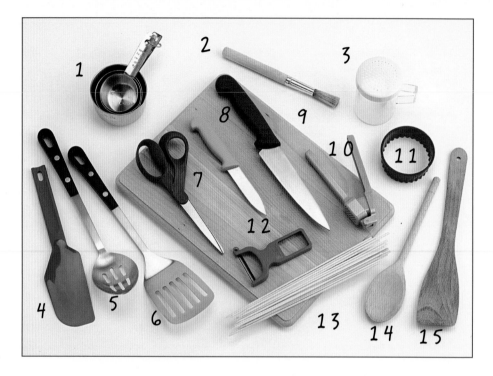

1 measuring cups

2 pastry brush

3 flour shaker

4 plastic spatula

5 slotted spoon

6 fish slice

7 scissors

8 sharp knives

9 chopping board

10 garlic crusher

11 cookie cutter

12 vegetable peeler

13 wooden skewers

14 wooden spoon

15 wooden spatula

Some recipes are more difficult than others and need lots of ingredients. All the recipes in this book are graded as

EASY

NOT SO EASY

DIFFICULT

(you may need some adult help for these recipes)

Cooking Tips

Read through the recipe and make sure you have bought all the necessary ingredients.

Check through the equipment list for each recipe before you start.

Here are a few useful tips about some of the
basic cooking skills that you will use for
the recipes in this book.

FOLDING IN

Using a metal spoon or a plastic
spatula, carefully fold one
mixture into another until all the
ingredients are mixed together.

MELTING

When melting chocolate, make
sure the bottom of the bowl
doesn't touch the water in the
pan. If the chocolate gets too hot,
it will be spoiled!

ROLLING OUT

When rolling out pastry, lightly
flour the surface and the rolling
pin. Roll out the pastry gently,
without stretching it.

LINING A TIN

Line the tin with baking paper
when making cakes, brownies
or flapjacks. It stops the cakes
sticking to the tin.

WHISKING

You whisk air into egg whites or cream to make them lighter. An electric hand mixer is a help, but a balloon whisk will also do the job.

KNEADING

You knead bread dough to make it stretchy so it will hold in air when cooking. Pull and stretch the dough with your hands, until smooth.

SEPARATING EGGS

Crack the shell and pour the egg on to a saucer. Place an eggcup over the yolk and pour the white into a bowl. Use the yolk as needed.

RUBBING IN

When making pastry or scones, you rub the butter and flour between your fingertips until the mixture looks like breadcrumbs.

WHAT YOU NEED:

Crudités
- 4 carrots, peeled
- 2 courgettes
- 4 sticks of celery
- half a cucumber
- 1 red pepper
- 1 yellow pepper
- 8 baby sweetcorn

Hummus
- 400 g canned chickpeas, drained
- juice of a lemon
- 2 cloves of garlic, crushed
- 2 tbsp tahini (sesame paste)
- 125 ml olive oil
- salt and freshly ground black pepper
- freshly chopped parsley and paprika to decorate

Cheesy Dip
- 250 g cream cheese
- 2 tbsp milk
- 2 spring onions, finely chopped
- 1 tbsp freshly chopped parsley
- 1 tbsp chives
- salt and freshly ground black pepper

WHAT TO USE:
- chopping board
- sharp knife
- mixing bowl
- wooden spoon
- food processor
- tablespoon
- serving plate
- 2 small bowls
- measuring jug

Sticks and Dips

Crudités (sticks of raw vegetables) are fab finger food – great for lunch boxes, parties or just when you have the munchies! Chunky sticks of crisp vegetables with dreamy flavoured dips – m'mmmm!

step one

1. Cut the carrots, courgettes and celery into sticks 6 cm long. Halve the cucumber, remove the seeds and cut into equal-sized sticks.

step two

2. Halve the peppers and remove the seeds. Cut each half into long strips.

step three

3. Make the cheesy dip by mixing the cheese and milk until smooth. Add the other ingredients and season.

step four

4. To make the hummus, blend the chickpeas, lemon juice and garlic in the processor. Add the tahini and blend until smooth.

step five

5. Keep the machine running and add the oil, a little at a time. Season.

step six

6. Put the dip and hummus in small bowls. Sprinkle the hummus with parsley and paprika. Put the bowls on a plate with the crudités around them.

For a change!
Dip 'n' dunk with crisps, bread sticks, crackers or other savoury biscuits for maximum fun!

15

2 | **5** minutes | **0** minutes

WHAT YOU NEED:

Berry Smoothie
- 1 small banana
- 150 g fresh raspberries and strawberries
- 300 ml milk
- caster sugar if required

Yoghurt Smoothie
- 1 small banana
- 1 ripe pear
- 200 ml apple juice
- 200 ml natural yoghurt
- 1 tsp vanilla extract
- 1 tbsp runny honey

WHAT TO USE:
- chopping board
- sharp knife
- teaspoon
- blender or food processor
- measuring jug

Fruit Smoothies

Check out these delicious fruit smoothies, which you can mix up in minutes. Simply choose any of your favourite fruits and get creative with different mixtures to make some really zany drinks!

For a change!
You can add crushed ice or ice cream to your smoothie to make a cooler drink for hot summer days.

16

Berry Smoothie

step one

1. For the berry smoothie, slice the banana. Halve the strawberries if they are very large.

step two

2. Place the fruit in the blender. Pour in the milk. Make sure the lid is on tight and blend until smooth.

step three

3. Taste and add sugar if required. Pour into smoothie glasses and serve with straws.

Yoghurt Smoothie

step one

1. For the yoghurt smoothie, slice the banana. Peel, core and chop the pear.

step two

2. Place all the ingredients in the blender. Make sure the lid is on tight and blend until smooth.

step three

3. Pour into smoothie glasses and serve.

WHAT YOU NEED:
- 2 large pitta breads

Filling
- 110 g canned tuna, drained
- 2 spring onions
- 110 g canned sweetcorn, drained
- 2 tbsp mayonnaise
- salt and freshly ground black pepper
- 2 eggs
- 2 little gem lettuces

WHAT TO USE
- chopping board
- sharp knife
- mixing bowl
- fork
- wooden spoon
- small saucepan
- slotted spoon
- tablespoon
- clingfilm or foil

Pitta

This recipe is easy and great fun! You can use pitta breads to make some really crazy sarnies, adding almost anything you like as a filling.

For a change!

Mix cold cooked chicken with mayonnaise and shredded lettuce. Spice up your mayonnaise by adding a little curry powder and a teaspoon of apricot jam.

For a veggie sarnie, use cream cheese mixed with chopped chives, baby spinach leaves and cherry tomatoes cut in half.

step one

1. Warm the pitta breads under the grill or in the oven. Cut each pitta in half to make two pouches.

step two

2. In a mixing bowl, flake the tuna with a fork. Finely chop the spring onions and add to the bowl.

step three

3. Add the sweetcorn and mayonnaise and mix together. Season well.

step four

4. Boil the eggs in a small saucepan for 10 minutes. Cool under cold running water. Peel and roughly chop the eggs and add to the mix.

step five

5. Wash and slice the lettuce. Place inside each pitta pouch.

step six

6. Spoon in the savoury filling. Eat now or wrap in clingfilm or foil until needed.

4 | **15** minutes | **70–90** minutes

WHAT YOU NEED:
- 4 large potatoes, about 250 g each
- 55 g butter
- salt and freshly ground black pepper
- 115 g ham
- 115 g Cheddar cheese

WHAT TO USE:
- fork
- baking tray
- dessert spoon
- mixing bowl
- sharp knife
- chopping board
- grater

Jacket Potatoes

For a lazy evening in front of the television, hot jacket potatoes are a great meal. Stuff them with your favourite fillings and eat them piping hot!

For a change!
For a veggie option, try some fried mushrooms instead of the ham.

Add flaked canned tuna or salmon to the mashed potato instead of the ham.

For an extra tasty meal, halve the hot potatoes and pour over some minced chilli sauce or bolognese sauce. Sprinkle with cheese to finish.

step one

1. Preheat the oven to 200°C/gas mark 6. Wash and wipe the potatoes. Prick with a fork and place on a baking tray.

step two

2. Cook the potatoes in the oven for 60–75 minutes until they are soft inside and the skins are crisp. Remove them from the oven.

step three

3. Cut each potato in half and scoop out the soft insides into the mixing bowl. Take care not to damage the skins.

step four

4. Mash the potato well with the fork. Add the butter and season.

step five

5. Place the skins on the baking tray. Chop the ham and put some into each shell. Spoon in the potato.

step six

6. Grate the cheese and sprinkle on the potatoes. Put them back in the oven and cook for a further 15 minutes until the tops are golden brown.

WHAT YOU NEED:

- 1 red and 1 yellow pepper
- 2 skinless chicken breast fillets
- 2 tbsp olive oil
- 2 tsp mild chilli powder
- 1 tsp paprika
- juice and grated rind of 1 lime
- salt and freshly ground black pepper
- 4 soft flour tortillas
- 55 g shredded iceberg lettuce
- 4 tbsp soured cream or plain yogurt

Spicy Tomato and Avocado Sauce

- 2 tomatoes, deseeded and chopped
- small red onion, very finely chopped
- 1 tbsp lime juice
- 1 tbsp olive oil
- 1 avocado, peeled, stoned and diced
- 1 tbsp chopped fresh coriander

WHAT TO USE:

- sharp knife
- chopping board
- non-metallic dish
- wooden spoon
- clingfilm
- bowl
- fork
- frying pan
- slotted spoon
- large serving plate
- 2 small bowls

Spicy Wraps

These spicy wraps, called fajitas, taste sensational! They come from Mexico and are soft tortillas filled with meat, salad and some spicy sauce. You'll have a fab time making them!

step one

1. Halve the peppers, remove the seeds and cut into long strips. Cut the chicken fillets into strips and place in a non-metallic dish.

step two

2. Add half the oil, the spices and lime juice and rind. Season. Mix together until the chicken is well coated. Cover and leave in the fridge for 1 hour.

step three

3. To make the spicy tomato and avocado sauce, mix together all the ingredients. Season, cover and keep cool.

step four

4. Heat the remaining oil in a frying pan. Fry the chicken, stirring, for 3 minutes. Add the peppers and fry for 3 minutes, until the chicken is cooked.

step five

5. Remove pan from heat. Spoon out the chicken and peppers and keep warm. Heat the tortillas in the oven. Put the sauce and cream in bowls.

step six

6. To make a fajita, put some sauce and sour cream onto a tortilla. Add the chicken, peppers and lettuce. Roll up the fajita and eat it!

8 | **15** minutes + 1 hour marinating | **8–10** minutes

WHAT YOU NEED:

- 450 g boned leg of lamb
- 2 red onions
- 8 mushrooms
- 8 cherry tomatoes
- 8 bay leaves

Marinade
- 4 tbsp olive oil
- juice of 1 lemon
- 1 clove of garlic, crushed
- salt and freshly ground black pepper

WHAT TO USE:

- mixing bowl
- garlic crusher
- sharp knife
- chopping board
- clingfilm and foil
- 8 wooden skewers
- pastry brush
- tablespoon
- lemon squeezer
- slotted spoon
- plate
- cooking tongs

Fab and Funky Kebabs

Kebabs make a wicked snack at any time, but they're particularly good in the summer when they can be cooked on a barbecue. These instructions are for cooking under the grill, but they are just as yummy!

For a change!

Prawns and cubes of salmon can be used to make funky fish kebabs.

To make veggie kebabs, use onions, squares of red and yellow pepper, chunks of courgettes and aubergines, boiled new potatoes and whole small tomatoes. Add some honey to the marinade for extra tastiness!

step one

1. Mix together the marinade ingredients in a bowl. Cut the meat into 2-cm cubes.

step two

2. Add the meat to the bowl and stir well. Cover and leave in the fridge for 1–2 hours. Remove the meat from the bowl onto a plate.

step three

3. Peel the onions and cut into chunky wedges. Wash the tomatoes. Wipe the mushrooms. Soak the skewers in cold water for 30 minutes.

step four

4. Push alternate meat cubes, onions, mushrooms, tomatoes and bay leaves onto the skewers. (Take care not to prick your fingers.)

step five

5. Preheat the grill. Line the grill pan with foil. Place the kebabs on the grill pan and brush with the marinade.

step six

6. Grill for 8–10 minutes. Turn kebabs every 2 minutes to make sure they are cooked evenly. Serve with some salad and rice, or a jacket potato.

WHAT YOU NEED:
- 450 g strong white flour
- 1 tsp salt
- 1 x 7-g sachet easy-blend yeast
- 1 tbsp vegetable oil
- 350 ml warm water
- 2 tbsp flour for dusting
- 1 egg, beaten for glazing
- sesame or poppy seeds to decorate

WHAT TO USE:
- large mixing bowl
- wooden spoon
- measuring jug
- flour shaker
- chopping board
- knife
- baking sheet
- pastry brush
- cooling rack
- tea towel or clingfilm

Seeded Bread Rolls

Home-made bread rolls are a special treat. Nothing smells better than fresh bread straight from the oven. It's fun to make and delicious to eat!

For a change!
Use half white and half wholemeal flour to make brown rolls.

step one

1. Mix the flour, salt and yeast in a bowl. Add the oil and water. Stir to form a soft dough.

step two

2. Knead dough on a floured surface for 5–7 minutes until smooth and elastic. Place in the bowl, cover with clingfilm and leave in a warm place to rise.

step three

3. When the dough has doubled in size (about 1 hour), knead it again on a lightly floured surface until smooth. Divide the dough into 8 equal pieces.

Cook's tip!
To test that your bread is cooked, tap the base of each roll — you should hear a hollow sound. Remember to let your rolls cool before eating them!

step four

4. Shape half the dough into round rolls. Make the other half into cottage rolls with a small round shape on top. Place rolls on a baking sheet.

step five

5. Cover rolls with a tea towel. Leave to rise for 30 minutes, until the bread has doubled in size. Preheat the oven to 220°C/gas mark 7.

step six

6. Glaze the rolls with egg and decorate with seeds. Sprinkle with flour for a soft roll. Bake in the oven for 10–15 minutes until golden brown.

WHAT YOU NEED:

- 175 g plain flour
- pinch of salt
- 85 g butter (or a mixture of butter and vegetable shortening)
- 2–3 tbsp cold water to mix
- 2 eggs, beaten
- 60 g grated Cheddar cheese
- 2 rashers of bacon, chopped into small pieces
- 150 ml milk
- salt and freshly ground black pepper

WHAT TO USE:

- mixing bowl
- sieve
- tablespoon
- round-bladed knife
- flour shaker
- rolling pin
- 7.5-cm pastry cutter
- bun tin
- measuring jug
- fork
- small frying pan
- wooden spatula
- cooling rack

Tasty Tartlets

You'll have a fab time making these easy-peasy tasty tartlets. Get creative with your choice of fillings — anything goes! Don't forget that you can make sweet tartlets too!

For a change!
For a veggie option, fry some sliced leeks and place in the cases before adding the egg mixture.

Make sweet tarts using raspberry jam or lemon curd, or try open mince pies with mincemeat.

step one

1. Preheat the oven to 200°C/gas mark 6. Sieve the flour and salt into the bowl. Add the butter and rub it into the flour. It should look like breadcrumbs.

step two

2. Sprinkle on the water and stir the mixture with a knife to make it come together. Press the pastry into a ball – the bowl should be clean.

step three

3. On a lightly floured surface slightly flatten the pastry with your hand. Then roll out to form a rough circle about 3 mm thick.

step four

4. Grease the bun tin. Cut out the pastry circles and place in the tin.

step five

5. Fry the bacon in a frying pan until crisp. Mix together the eggs, cheese, bacon, milk and seasoning.

step six

6. Spoon the mixture into the cases. Bake in the oven for 15 minutes. Remove from the oven. Leave to cool slightly and then place on a wire rack.

WHAT YOU NEED:

- 1 onion
- 2 leeks
- 1 clove of garlic
- 450 g carrots
- 225 g parsnips
- 1 tbsp olive oil
- 25 g butter
- 850 ml vegetable stock
- grated rind and juice of 2 oranges
- salt and freshly ground black pepper
- 1 tbsp chopped fresh parsley

WHAT TO USE:

- chopping board
- sharp knife
- garlic crusher
- large saucepan plus lid
- wooden spatula
- measuring jug
- hand-held blender
- warm soup bowls
- grater
- lemon squeezer

Soup

For a cosy meal on a cold day, soup is just fab. You can feed all your family and friends with this tasty recipe – the more, the merrier!

step one

1. Peel the onion and leeks and chop finely. Peel the garlic and crush. Peel the carrots and parsnips and chop into cubes.

step two

2. Heat the oil and butter in the saucepan over medium heat. Add the onion and garlic and fry gently for 2–3 minutes.

step three

3. Add the remaining vegetables and continue to cook for a further 2 minutes.

step four

4. Pour in the stock. Cover with a tightly fitting lid and simmer over low heat for 15–20 minutes.

step five

5. Remove the pan from the heat. Blend the soup until smooth.

step six

6. Add the orange juice. Taste and season well. Serve the soup in warm bowls. Garnish with the orange rind and some chopped parsley.

For a change!

If you like a chunky soup do not blend the cooked mixture.

Make green soup by using 350 g spinach instead of the carrots and parsnips. Flavour with nutmeg and finish off by swirling in some cream.

For a tasty topping, sprinkle on some grated cheese before serving.

Risotto

When you're in a big rush, risotto is a great way to beat the clock and fill your tum! This recipe is for a whole meal to be served in one dish.

step one

1. Place the rice in the pan and add the stock. Bring to boil and stir. Cover and cook over low heat for 11–12 minutes.

step two

2. While the rice is cooking, heat the oil in the frying pan. Fry the bacon and onion until the bacon is cooked and the onion soft.

step three

3. Add the red pepper and mushrooms and continue to cook for 2–3 minutes.

step four

4. Add the peas and sweetcorn and heat through.

step five

5. When the rice is cooked (check the pack instructions), remove pan from the heat. Gently fork through the rice to separate the grains.

step six

6. Turn the rice into a heated serving dish and add the contents of the frying pan. Mix together gently. Sprinkle with the parsley.

For a change!

For a vegetarian option, leave out the bacon and serve with some grated cheese.

For a more substantial meal add 225 g chopped cooked chicken to the rice.

Make yellow risotto by adding ¼ tsp turmeric to the stock. Add 2 chopped spring onions for extra taste.

WHAT YOU NEED:
- 250 g pasta shapes
- $^1/_4$ tsp salt
- 55 g butter
- 40 g plain flour
- 450 ml milk
- 125 g Cheddar cheese, grated
- salt and freshly ground black pepper
- 125 g cooked ham, roughly chopped
- 25 g Parmesan cheese, freshly grated
- 4 cherry tomatoes, cut into quarters

WHAT TO USE:
- large saucepan
- medium saucepan
- colander
- wooden spatula
- grater
- ovenproof dish
- baking tray

Pasta Bake

For a delicious dinner, pasta is the ultimate yummy food. A pasta bake is a brilliant way to make large amounts to feed all your friends. They'll love the gorgeous sauce and crunchy topping!

For a change!
Add 115 g sweetcorn and 220 g canned tuna, drained and flaked, to the pasta.

step one

1. Preheat the oven to 200°C/ gas mark 6. Heat some water in the large saucepan. Add salt and bring to the boil.

step two

2. Add the pasta carefully, taking care not to splash. Cook the pasta according to the pack instructions.

step three

3. Gently melt the butter in a saucepan over a low heat. Add the flour and mix well. Cook mixture for 1 minute and then remove from the heat.

step four

4. Stir in the milk, a little at a time, to make a smooth sauce. Put pan back on heat. Stir while the sauce thickens so it doesn't go lumpy.

step five

5. When the sauce is boiling, turn down heat and cook, still stirring, for 1–2 minutes. Remove from heat. Mix in the Cheddar, ham and tomatoes. Season.

step six

6. Drain the pasta. Mix with the sauce. Place in an ovenproof dish and sprinkle with Parmesan. Bake in the oven, on a baking tray, for 25–30 minutes.

WHAT YOU NEED:

- 450 g minced beef
- 1 onion, finely chopped
- 1 egg, beaten
- salt and freshly ground black pepper
- 1 tbsp flour for shaping
- 1 tbsp olive oil

To Serve

- 4–6 burger buns
- half a lettuce
- 2 tomatoes
- mustard, ketchup or mayonnaise

WHAT TO USE:

- mixing bowl
- fork
- chopping board
- grill pan
- pastry brush
- cooking tongs
- sharp knife

Best-ever Burgers

You can have a fab time making these tasty burgers using both meat and vegetables. Make them even more yummy by adding your favourite sauce!

step one

1. Put the mince in the mixing bowl and add the onion, egg and seasoning. Mix well.

step two

2. Lightly flour your hands and the chopping board. Divide the mixture into 4–6 equal portions and shape into burgers.

step three

3. Chill the burgers in the fridge for 10 minutes. Preheat the grill. Place the chilled burgers on the grill pan and brush with oil.

step four

4. Grill the burgers for 4–6 minutes. Turn the burgers over, brush again with oil. Grill for a further 4–6 minutes until done.

step five

5. Cut the buns in half. Toast them under the hot grill, if you wish. Slice the tomatoes thinly. Wash and shred the lettuce.

step six

6. Place a handful of lettuce in each bun, then add the burger. Garnish with a slice of tomato. Serve with your choice of sauce.

For a change!
To make veggie burgers, you will need:
2 400-g cans of cannellini beans, drained and rinsed
2 tbsp chopped parsley or coriander
grated rind of 1 lemon
1 beaten egg

Mix altogether in a blender. Season well and shape the mixture into 4 even-sized burgers. Chill for 1–2 hours and then fry in a non-stick frying pan for 5 minutes on each side.
Serve with salad.

4 | **15** minutes + rising | **15–20** minutes

WHAT YOU NEED:

Base

- 225 g strong white flour
- $1/2$ tsp salt
- 2 tsp easy-blend yeast
- 1 tbsp vegetable oil
- 175 ml warm water
- 2 tbsp flour for dusting

Topping

- 400 g canned chopped tomatoes
- 2 tbsp tomato purée
- 2 tsp dried oregano
- salt and freshly ground black pepper
- 2 slices of ham, torn into bite-sized pieces
- 150 g mozzarella cheese, torn into bite-sized pieces
- 2 tbsp olive oil
- 1 yellow pepper, sliced
- 4 button mushrooms sliced
- fresh basil leaves

WHAT TO USE:

- large mixing bowl
- wooden spoon
- measuring jug
- flour shaker
- chopping board
- rolling pin
- clingfilm
- knife
- 2 baking sheets (greased)
- sieve
- bowl

Pizzas to Go!

Feeling lazy but got the munchies? Then pizza is a brilliant idea for an easy meal. Making these mini pizzas is loads of floury fun – and everyone can choose their favourite topping.

step one

1. Make the dough following the instructions for bread on page 16, up to the end of step 3.

step two

2. Flour your hands and the work surface. Knead the dough until smooth. Stretch into shape and roll thinly into two circles, 15 cm across.

step three

3. Pinch up the edges of the dough. Grease the baking sheets. Place the bases on the sheets and leave them to rise while you make the topping.

step four

4. Preheat the oven to 220°C/gas mark 7. Drain the tomatoes and put into a bowl with the purée and oregano. Mix and season.

step five

5. Spread half the mixture over each base. Arrange the ham, cheese, pepper and mushrooms on top. Brush over the olive oil.

step six

6. Bake in the oven for 15–20 minutes until the crusts are pale golden and firm. Remove from the oven. Decorate with basil and serve.

WHAT YOU NEED:

- 2 fillets of plaice or other white fish, skinned and cut into 2-cm-wide strips
- salt and pepper
- 2 tbsp plain flour
- 1 egg
- 115 g white or wholemeal breadcrumbs
- 1 tbsp finely chopped fresh parsley
- 2 large potatoes, scrubbed
- 6 tbsp olive oil

To Serve

- half a lemon, cut into segments
- ketchup or mayonnaise

WHAT TO USE:

- cook's knife
- chopping board
- plate
- bowl
- fork
- shallow dish
- plastic bag
- 2 baking trays
- pastry brush
- cooking tongs
- fish slice

Crunchy Fish and Chips

Wow! With this funky recipe you can make your very own take-away food at home. The fish is coated with breadcrumbs, giving it the crunchiest, crumbliest coating!

step one

1. Preheat the oven to 200°C/ gas mark 6. Season the flour and put on a plate. Roll the strips of fish in the flour until covered.

step two

2. Beat the egg in a bowl and pour it into a shallow dish. Dip the fish into the beaten egg. Mix the parsley and breadcrumbs. Season.

step three

3. Put the mixture into a plastic bag and toss in the fish to coat thoroughly. Chill on a baking tray in the fridge for 30 minutes.

step four

4. Cut each potato into 8 wedges. Place on a baking tray and brush over half the oil. Turn the potatoes to coat them all over. Season.

step five

5. Bake the chips for 35–40 minutes until golden, turning occasionally. After 20 minutes remove the fish from fridge. Drizzle with the rest of the oil.

step six

6. Bake at the top of the oven for 15–20 minutes, turning halfway through. Serve with the lemon and your favourite sauce.

WHAT YOU NEED:

- 100 g plain flour
- pinch of salt
- 1 egg, beaten
- 300 ml milk
- 10 tsp butter or oil

To Serve
- lemon juice
- caster sugar

WHAT TO USE:

- sieve
- mixing bowl
- wooden spoon
- measuring jug
- 18-cm non-stick frying pan
- teaspoon
- plate
- wooden spatula
- baking paper and foil

Perfect Pancakes

Why wait for Pancake Day? These tasty treats can be mixed up in moments at any time. You can add different toppings, from sugar, maple syrup or honey with lemon juice to lashings of delicious chocolate sauce!

For a change!
Serve your pancakes with warmed honey or jam. Or try them with sliced bananas and runny chocolate sauce.

Go savoury and layer up the pancakes with meat or vegetable fillings. Serve with a topping of melted grated cheese.

step one

1. Sieve the flour and salt in the bowl. Make a 'well' in the centre; add the egg and half the milk. Beat the egg and milk together.

step two

2. Gradually mix in the flour. When the mixture is smooth with no lumps, beat in the rest of the milk. Carefully pour the mixture into the jug.

step three

3. Heat the pan over a medium heat. Add a teaspoon of the butter or oil and swirl it around to cover the whole surface.

Serve them hot!
Serve the pancakes while they're still hot. Sprinkle with the lemon juice and sugar and roll them up.

step four

4. Pour in enough batter to cover the base. Swirl around the pan while tilting it so you have a thin, even layer. Cook for about 30 seconds.

step five

5. Lift up the edge of the pancake to see if it is brown. Loosen round the edges and flip with the spatula. Cook the other side until golden brown.

step six

6. Turn out each pancake onto a warm plate. Stack in layers with baking paper. Cover with foil and keep warm.

30–40
minutes

1–2
hours

WHAT YOU NEED

- 8 trifle sponges and 100 g strawberry jam or 1 Swiss roll
- 125 ml orange juice (or juice from a can of fruit)
- 40 g macaroons or ratafias
- 350 g fresh strawberries or other fruit (fresh or canned)

Custard

- 425 ml single cream
- 5 egg yolks
- 3 tbsp caster sugar
- $1/2$ tsp vanilla extract

Topping

- 300 ml double cream
- 2 tbsp milk
- chocolate flakes to decorate

WHAT TO USE:

- chopping board
- sharp knife
- mixing bowl
- balloon whisk
- clingfilm
- saucepan
- wooden spoon
- measuring jug
- 6 glass bowls

Gorgeous Trifle

With lashings of yummy custard and cream, trifle is a wicked treat for special days. You can add almost anything you like for a delicious topping sensation – m'mmmmmm!

step one

1. Cut the sponges into pieces and spread with the jam (or just slice the Swiss roll). Place in the bowls and pour over the fruit juice.

step two

2. Add the macaroons to the bowls and spoon the fruit on top. Cream together the egg yolks, sugar and vanilla extract in a jug.

step three

3. Heat the single cream in a saucepan until just before boiling point. Pour the hot cream into the jug, stirring all the time until mixed.

step four

4. Put the mixture back into the pan. Heat gently, stirring constantly, until the sauce has thickened enough to coat the back of a spoon.

step five

5. Put the base of the pan in cold water and stir until cool. Spoon the custard over the trifle. Cover with clingfilm and chill in the fridge for 1–2 hours.

step six

6. Just before serving, whip the double cream with the milk until it is thick but soft. Spoon over the custard. Decorate and serve chilled.

WHAT YOU NEED:

- 55 g butter
- 4 tbsp golden syrup
- 100 g milk chocolate, broken into pieces
- 70 g cornflakes

WHAT TO USE:

- mixing bowl
- large saucepan
- wooden spoon
- dessert spoon
- knife
- bun tin
- 12 paper cases
- cake tin for storage

Chocolate Crispie Cakes

This is an easy-peasy recipe — it's probably one of the very first recipes you'll make. These scrunchy, chewy little cakes are delicious at any time — and they need almost no cooking.

step one

1. Put the butter, syrup and chocolate in the mixing bowl. Place the bowl over a large saucepan of simmering water.

step two

2. Allow the butter, syrup and chocolate to melt, stirring to mix well.

step three

3. Remove the pan from the heat. Take the bowl out of the saucepan.

step four

4. Add the cornflakes to the mixture and stir well, using the wooden spoon.

step five

5. Carefully spoon the mixture into the paper cases. Take care you don't make the cases too messy.

step six

6. Leave your crispies to set in the fridge for 1 hour. You can store them in an airtight tin so they stay crisp.

For a change!

You can use puffed wheat or rice crispies instead of the cornflakes.

You could use dark chocolate or even white if you like.

Add 55 g raisins to make even chewier crispie cakes.

Peppermint Creams

24 | 30 minutes | 1 hour

WHAT YOU NEED:
- 1 egg white
- 350 g white icing sugar + extra for shaping
- 3 drops peppermint essence
- 2 drops green food colouring
- 125 g dark chocolate, broken into pieces

WHAT TO USE:
- mixing bowl
- balloon whisk
- sieve
- wooden spoon
- chopping board
- teaspoon
- baking tray lined with non-stick paper
- fork
- small saucepan
- heatproof bowl

These scrummy peppermint creams make great presents for mums, dads, grandparents – even best friends. They are easy to make, and you'll have fun dipping them in the chocolate. Don't eat all the sweets while making them!

Gift wrapped!
Arrange your peppermint creams in a prettily decorated box or tin lined with coloured tissue paper. Your granny or teacher will love them!

step one

1. Whisk the egg white until frothy. Sieve in the icing sugar and mix well. Add the peppermint essence and the colouring and mix well.

step two

2. Sprinkle icing sugar onto your hands. Roll teaspoon-sized amounts of the mixture into small balls and place on the baking tray.

step three

3. Flatten each ball with a fork to form flat discs. Place in the fridge for 1 hour until firm.

48

step four

4. Put the chocolate pieces into the heatproof bowl. Place the bowl on a pan of simmering water (about 5 cm deep).

step five

5. When the chocolate has melted, remove from the heat and stir until smooth. Allow to cool a little.

step six

6. Dip each sweet into the chocolate until half covered. Place sweets on the non-stick paper to set. Keep in a cool place or a fridge until needed.

4 | **15–20** minutes | **2** hours

WHAT YOU NEED:
- 125 g plain chocolate, broken into pieces
- 4 large eggs
- 50 g white chocolate

WHAT TO USE:
- heatproof bowl
- saucepan
- tablespoon
- mixing bowl
- saucer
- eggcup
- small bowl
- teaspoon
- electric hand mixer or balloon whisk
- flexible spatula
- grater
- 4 small serving dishes

Double Chocolate Mousse

This mousse is lots of fun to make! Learn how to melt chocolate and whisk egg whites while making a really groovy pud!

step one

1. Put the chocolate in the heatproof bowl. Place bowl on a pan of simmering water (5 cm deep) and allow the chocolate to melt.

step two

2. Separate the eggs following the method described on page 13. Pour the egg whites into the mixing bowl and put the yolks in the small bowl.

step three

3. Remove the melted chocolate from the heat and stir well. Cool a little. Beat the yolks and slowly add them to the chocolate, stirring well.

For a change!

For a zingy 'chocolate orange' flavour, add grated orange zest to the melted chocolate.

For a crunchy surprise, add some chopped nuts in the bottom of the serving dishes before adding the mousse.

step four

4. Whisk the egg whites in the mixing bowl until they are white and firm and will stand up in soft peaks.

step five

5. With the spatula, gently fold the whites into the chocolate and egg yolk mixture until evenly mixed.

step six

6. Carefully pour the mousse into the serving dishes and leave to set in the fridge for 2 hours. Decorate with grated white chocolate.

(18) 🍽️

🥣 10–15 minutes

🍳 25–30 minutes

WHAT YOU NEED:
- 175 g butter
- 125 g soft light-brown sugar
- 55 g golden syrup
- 350 g porridge oats

WHAT TO USE:
- rectangular cake tin 20 x 30 cm, greased and lined with baking paper
- large saucepan
- wooden spoon
- flexible spatula
- round-bladed knife
- cooling rack
- cake tin for storage

Munchy Flapjacks

Flapjacks are a really scrummy treat for when you have the munchies! They taste great and, as they are made from oats, they're good for you too!

For a change!

You can add 70 g raisins to make fruity flapjacks. For an extra-healthy option, add 55 g chopped dates and 55 g sunflower seeds. Try using honey instead of syrup.

For a fab treat, melt 55 g dark chocolate and dip the flapjacks to coat the top. Cool on a wire rack while the chocolate sets.

step one

1. Preheat the oven to 180°C/gas mark 4. Put the butter, sugar and syrup into the saucepan.

step two

2. Heat pan over a low heat for 2–3 minutes, stirring until melted. Remove the pan from the hob, add the porridge oats and mix.

step three

3. Pour the mixture into the prepared cake tin. Press down well using a spatula.

step four

4. Bake in the centre of the oven for 25–30 minutes until golden but still slightly soft. Remove from the oven and leave to cool for 10 minutes.

step five

5. Cut into squares and allow to cool completely in the tin.

step six

6. Carefully remove the flapjacks from the tin using a knife. Store in an airtight container for up to 1 week.

WHAT YOU NEED:
- 125 g butter
- 125 g golden caster sugar
- 1 large egg, beaten
- 1 ripe banana, mashed
- 175 g self-raising flour
- 1 tsp mixed spice
- 2 tbsp milk
- 100 g chopped mixed nuts
- 55 g raisins

WHAT TO USE:
- mixing bowl
- wooden spoon or electric hand mixer
- small bowl
- fork
- sieve
- flexible spatula
- dessert spoon
- 2 baking trays lined with baking paper
- round-bladed knife
- cooling rack
- cake tin for storage

Mini Cookies

These bite-sized delights are great snacks. The only problem is that everyone will love them, so don't be surprised if they all get eaten very quickly!

For a change!
You can replace the nuts with 100 g of chocolate cut into chunks — m'mmm!

Make dreamy peanut butter cookies by adding 2 tablespoons of peanut butter instead of the banana. Use chopped peanuts instead of the mixed nuts. Leave out the spice and raisins.

step one

1. Preheat the oven to 190°C/gas mark 5. Cream together the butter and sugar with a wooden spoon or mixer until light and fluffy.

step two

2. Add the egg gradually to the mixture, beating well each time. Mash the banana and add it in, beating until the mixture is smooth.

step three

3. Sieve in the flour and spice. Fold in using a spatula. Add the milk to give a soft consistency. Fold in the nuts and fruit.

step four

step five

step six

4. Drop dessert spoons of the mixture onto the lined baking trays. Space cookies well apart (about 9 on each tray).

5. Bake in the centre of the oven for 15–20 minutes until lightly golden.

6. Remove from the oven and leave to firm up slightly. Transfer to a cooling rack using a round-bladed knife. Allow to cool before storing.

12

20 minutes

25 minutes

WHAT YOU NEED:

- 175 g dark chocolate, broken into pieces
- 175 g butter
- 250 g golden caster sugar
- pinch of salt
- 3 large eggs
- 115 g plain flour
- 2 tsp vanilla extract
- 100 g chocolate chips

WHAT TO USE:

- 20-cm square cake tin
- non-stick baking paper
- scissors
- heatproof bowl
- saucepan
- wooden spoon
- small bowl
- fork
- sieve
- flexible spatula
- knife
- teaspoon

Brownies

Brownies are the best! They're soft and gooey on the inside, and crisp on the outside – delicious! For extra crunch value you could add some chopped nuts.

step one

1. Preheat the oven to 180°C/gas mark 4. Grease the cake tin and line it with non-stick baking paper.

step two

2. Place the chocolate and butter in a bowl. Melt over a pan of simmering water. Stir until smooth. Remove pan from the heat. Cool slightly.

step three

3. Add the sugar and salt to the melted chocolate. Beat the eggs in a bowl and add them gradually to the mixture.

step four

4. Sift the flour into the mixture and beat until smooth. Add the vanilla extract and stir in the chocolate chips.

step five

step six

5. Scrape the mixture into the tin. Bake for 20–25 minutes until the top is pale brown and the middle is soft. Remove from the oven.

6. Allow the brownies to cool in the tin before cutting into pieces. Remove from the tin and serve with ice cream to make a delicious dessert.

For a change!

You can use white chocolate chips or chopped walnuts as an alternative.

You can serve your brownie squares as party cakes with an individual candle on each brownie.

WHAT YOU NEED:

- 125 g butter (softened at room temperature)
- 125 g caster sugar
- 2 eggs, beaten
- 125 g self-raising flour
- 2 tbsp milk

Icing

- 225 g icing sugar
- 1 tbsp lemon juice
- 1 tbsp warm water

To Decorate

- sweets, chocolate buttons, hundreds and thousands, silver balls, grated coconut, glacé cherries

WHAT TO USE:

- mixing bowl
- wooden spoon
- sieve
- tablespoon
- muffin tin
- 12 paper cases
- cooling rack
- small bowl
- lemon squeezer
- teaspoon

Cupcake Treats

With their soft sponge middles and yummy icing topping, cupcakes are an all-time favourite teatime treat. You can make them any colour and decorate them in a funky way!

step one

1. Preheat the oven to 190°C/gas mark 5. Use a wooden spoon to cream the butter and sugar until light and fluffy.

step two

2. Add the eggs a little at a time, beating well after each addition. Sieve the flour into the bowl and carefully fold in using a tablespoon.

step three

3. Mix in the milk. Stir until the mixture is smooth and drops off the spoon easily. Divide the mixture between the paper cases (in the tin).

step four

4. Bake in the oven for 15–20 minutes until the cakes are risen and golden brown. Remove from the oven and put on a cooling rack.

step five

5. Sieve the icing sugar into the bowl. Add the lemon juice and stir in the warm water. Mix until thick and smooth.

step six

6. Spoon the icing onto the cakes. Spread to the case edges with the back of a teaspoon. Use your imagination to decorate!

For a change!
Get creative and make some funky colours of icing for your cupcakes. Divide the icing mixture into small bowls and add a different colour to each one.

WHAT YOU NEED:

Toffee Ice Cream
- 85 g golden syrup
- 85 g light muscovado sugar
- 55 g butter
- 1 tsp vanilla extract
- 140 ml double cream
- 500 g Greek-style yoghurt
- 100 g fudge, chopped into small pieces

Berry Ice Cream
- 150 ml fruit pureé, made from frozen pack of forest fruits, thawed
- 400-g carton of fresh custard
- 400 g fromage frais

WHAT TO USE:
- small saucepan
- wooden spoon
- mixing bowl
- balloon whisk
- flexible spatula
- 2 1.2-litre plastic freezer boxes with lids
- fork
- tablespoon

Ice Cream

You can make loads of these dreamy ice cream mixtures without even needing a special ice cream maker. Just follow these simple recipes and get scooping!

Toffee Ice Cream

step one

1. Place the syrup, sugar and butter in a pan over a low heat. Stir to dissolve the sugar and melt the butter. Take off the heat. Stir in the vanilla.

For a change!
Instead of the frozen forest fruits, you could use fresh raspberries or strawberries when in season.

step two

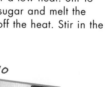

2. Beat the cream until soft and thick. Fold in the yoghurt, cooled toffee sauce and fudge. Pour the mixture into the box. Cover and freeze for 1 hour.

step three

3. Stir the frozen mixture and return to the freezer for 1 hour. Repeat until the mixture is frozen. Place in the fridge for 30 minutes before serving.

Berry Ice Cream

step four

step five

step six

1. Mash the thawed fruits with a fork until they form a purée.

2. Pour the yoghurt and the fromage frais into a mixing bowl. Carefully stir in the fruit purée using a spatula.

3. Pour the mixture into a plastic box. Cover and freeze for 1 hour. Follow the instructions in step 3 on the opposite page.

Cooking Words

beat
to mix ingredients together, using a wooden spoon or hand mixer, until soft and stretchy.

blend
to mix together, using a blender or food processor, to make a liquid or a smooth mix.

chop
to chop food into small pieces with a knife.

cream
to beat butter and sugar together using a wooden spoon or hand mixer; the creamed mixture should be smooth and pale.

drain
to pour off water from cooked foods, using a sieve or a colander.

drizzle
to pour a trickle of oil over the top of food.

fold in
to mix gently; use a metal spoon or spatula so that you don't remove the air beaten in earlier.

garnish
to decorate a savoury dish with whole or chopped herbs, chopped nuts, sliced tomatoes and so on.

glaze
to brush food with egg yolk or milk so that it looks shiny and golden when baked.

grease

to brush a baking tray or cake tin with oil or rub with butter to stop the food from sticking.

knead

to work with bread dough on a board so that it becomes smooth and elastic.

rise

to put bread dough in a warm place so the yeast can work; the dough should double in size.

rub in

to rub butter into flour, using the tips of your fingers, to produce a mixture that looks like breadcrumbs.

season

to add salt and pepper to food to increase its taste.

sieve

to use a sieve to drain liquid or to remove any lumps from sugar or flour before adding them to a mixture; sieving also adds air to the mix.

simmer

to cook a liquid in a pan so that it bubbles gently but does not boil.

whisk

to beat a mixture very hard to add air so that the mixture becomes thick; use either a balloon whisk or an electric hand mixer.

Index